CONTENTS

Whatever you choose to make first, you'll need plenty of packaging. So it's a good idea to start collecting it in advance. Ask people to save things for you instead of throwing them away.

You can flatten cardboard boxes and cereal boxes to save space. Rinse plastic bottles and leave them to dry. Prepare an area to work in, and have lots of old newspapers handy if you are using glue and paints.

HOW TO MAKE A TABULA

Children learned to write using a wax tablet called a **tabula**. This was a wooden board covered with a thin layer of beeswax. The letters were scratched on the wax surface with a sharp stick called a **stylus**. They were rubbed out by smoothing them over with the round end of the stylus, leaving the tablet fresh and ready to use again.

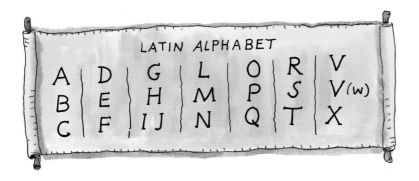

LATIN ALPHABET

A	D	G	L	O	R	V
B	E	H	M	P	S	V(w)
C	F	IJ	N	Q	T	X

LVCIA

IX

IX (age)

YOU'LL NEED:
Corrugated cardboard, rolling pin, plasticine, craft knife, scissors, glue, ruler, pencil, old ballpoint pen, paints, and brushes.

GRAFFITI
WRITING ON WALLS ISN'T NEW. THE ROMANS DID IT A LOT, OFTEN USING A CHISEL!

SPARTACVS INNOCENS EST VERITATE (Spartacus is innocent, Ok!)

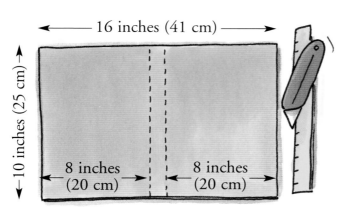

16 inches (41 cm)

10 inches (25 cm)

8 inches (20 cm)   8 inches (20 cm)

⭐ **1** Cut out a rectangle of corrugated cardboard.

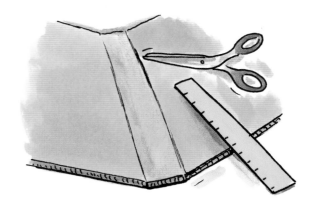

⭐ **2** Use the scissors to score two lines down the center 1/2 inch (1 cm) apart. Fold to make a spine.

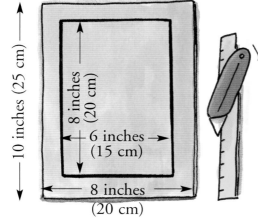

10 inches (25 cm)

8 inches (20 cm)

6 inches (15 cm)

8 inches (20 cm)

⭐ **3** Cut out another cardboard rectangle. Cut out the center to form a frame.

⭐ **4** Glue this to the right-hand side of the first rectangle.

⭐ **5** Roll some plasticine flat and fill the frame with it.

⭐ **6** Decorate the front of the **tabula** using your stencils and mosaics (see page 6). Use the old ballpoint pen as a **stylus**. Rub out with the plastic cap.

HOW TO MAKE AN ABACUS

Roman numbers were based on the hand. One finger was held up for 1 and one hand for 5, written as the letter V. Two hands were 10, written as two Vs, like this: Λ. This became the letter X. Later other letters were used for bigger numbers: L=50, C=100, D=500, M=1,000.

This system made adding really hard, so the Romans used a simple counting board called an **abacus** with small stones as hundreds, tens, and ones.

YOU'LL NEED:

Thin cardboard, 27 bottle tops or coins, ruler, pencil, glue, and scissors.

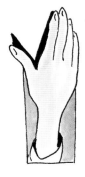

I	1	XVI	16
II	2	XVII	17
III	3	XVIII	18
IV	4	XIX	19
V	5	XX	20
VI	6	XXX	30
VII	7	XL	40
VIII	8	L	50
IX	9	LX	60
X	10	LXX	70
XI	11	LXXX	80
XII	12	XC	90
XIII	13	C	100
XIV	14	D	500
XV	15	M	1,000

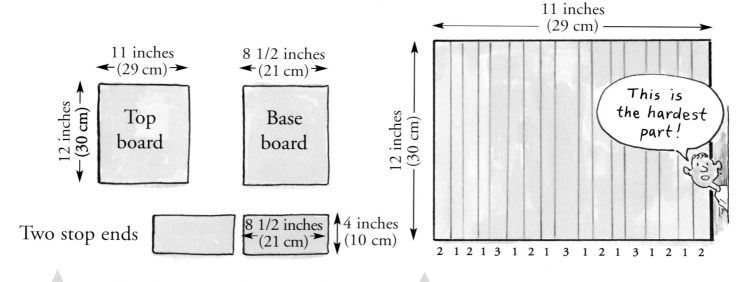

11 inches (29 cm) · **12 inches (30 cm)** — Top board

8 1/2 inches (21 cm) — Base board

Two stop ends — **8 1/2 inches (21 cm)** · **4 inches (10 cm)**

11 inches (29 cm) · **12 inches (30 cm)**

2 1 2 1 3 1 2 1 3 1 2 1 3 1 2 1 2

This is the hardest part!

1 ⭐ Cut these out of thin cardboard.

2 ⭐ Very carefully mark out the top board (measured in cm).

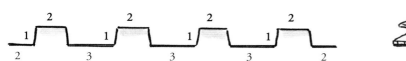

2 · 1 · 1 · 1 · 1 · 2
2 · 3 · 3 · 3 · 2

3 ⭐ Fold the top board like this (measured in cm).

4 ⭐ Glue it to the baseboard.

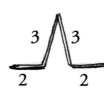

2
3
3
2

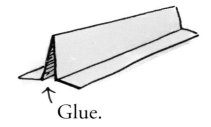

3 3
2   2

Glue.

5 ⭐ Fold and glue the two stop ends (measured in cm).

Glue.

6 ⭐ Glue the stop ends to each side of the board.

7 ⭐ Put nine bottle tops or coins in each of the three grooves (for hundreds, tens, and ones) and start counting!

V **5**

HOW TO MAKE A MOSAIC

Roman mosaics are famous. They are pictures made up of thousands of tiny pieces of colored stone or tile fixed in cement. They were used to decorate the floors of Roman villas. You can see them in museums all over the world.

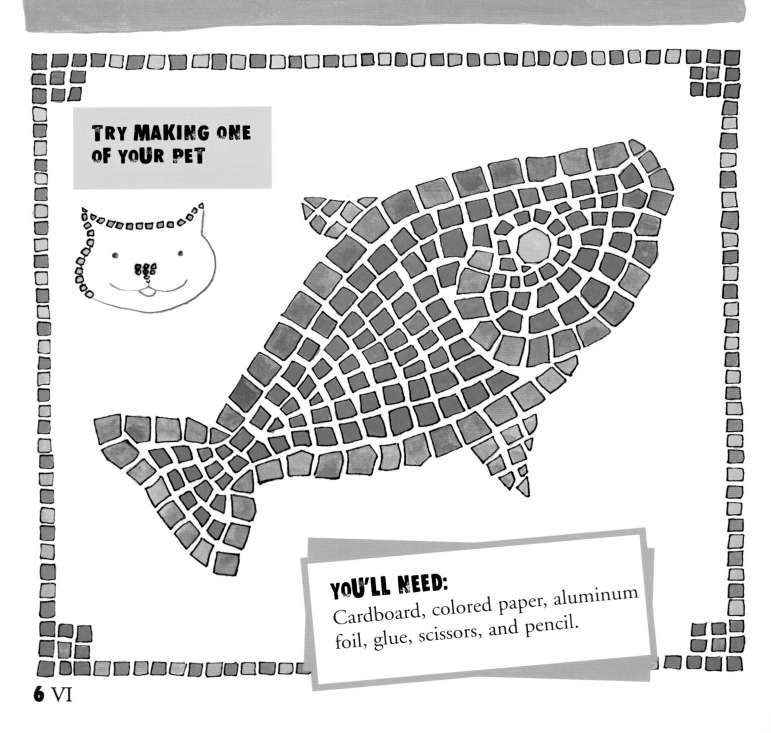

TRY MAKING ONE OF YOUR PET

YOU'LL NEED:
Cardboard, colored paper, aluminum foil, glue, scissors, and pencil.

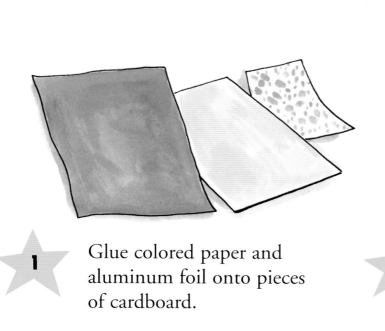

1 Glue colored paper and aluminum foil onto pieces of cardboard.

2 Then cut the cardboard into small shapes like this.

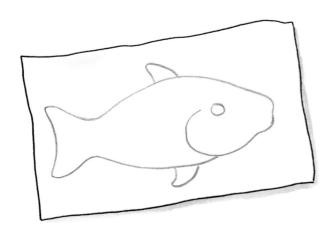

3 Draw an outline of your design on a piece of paper or cardboard.

TIP BOX
Use empty yogurt containers to store the colored shapes.

BLUE

RED

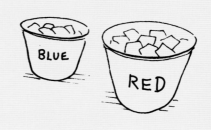

4 Glue the small shapes onto your design. You can trim them to fit.

HOW TO MAKE A ROMAN BORDER

Beautiful mosaics were often surrounded by a black-and-white border. The Romans used simple shapes and repeated them to make patterns. They were always worked out first on a grid. Graph paper makes this easy. Have a look at the ideas on the opposite page. You could try them or experiment and make up your own designs. Beware, sometimes the squares make your eyes go funny!

YOU'LL NEED:
Graph paper, black felt-tips, black-and-white paint and brushes or crayons, ruler, and pencil.

TIP BOX
Copy the design by marking the squares in pencil with a "b" for black. These will be hidden when you paint over them.

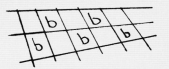

1 Draw all the vertical and horizontal lines at one time to save moving your ruler. If in doubt, mark anything with pencil first. The felt-tip or paint will easily go over it. Any grid lines showing can also be painted over.

2 Make a bold edge for the finished work by going around with a thick black line.

HOW TO MAKE A TOGA

Roman men who were citizens wore a **toga**. It was a large semicircle of woolen cloth draped around the body with a tunic (**tunica**) worn underneath. An emperor's **toga** could be 20 feet (6 m) long and was dyed bright purple. Women wore a dress called a **stola**. They preferred linen or cotton to wool. Very rich people wore silk specially imported all the way from China.

TOGS IS A SLANG WORD FOR CLOTHES

YOU'LL NEED:
An old white double sheet, an extra-large white T-shirt, 3 feet (1 m) of string, thumbtack, scissors, and pencil.

SUBLIGACULUM IS LATIN FOR ROMAN UNDERPANTS

Insert the thumbtack halfway across the sheet.

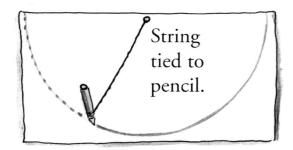

String tied to pencil.

1 Mark out a semicircle on the sheet using the string and thumbtack. Cut it out.

2 Put on the T-shirt, and use the string as a belt.

3 Hang one end of the **toga** over your left shoulder.

4 Now toss the other end over the top of it.

5 Tuck the middle into the string belt.

TIP BOX
Never mind if you have a mishap with your **toga**—as long as you're wearing your **subligaculum**!

THE ROMAN EMPIRE

The 2nd century AD

BC

753 BC	**509 BC ROME**	**264–146 BC**	**44–27 BC**
The legendary founding of Rome by Romulus, the first king.	Rome becomes a republic.	Wars with Carthage, a rival power in North Africa.	Julius Caesar is made dictator for life and then murdered. Rome becomes an empire. Augustus is the first emperor.

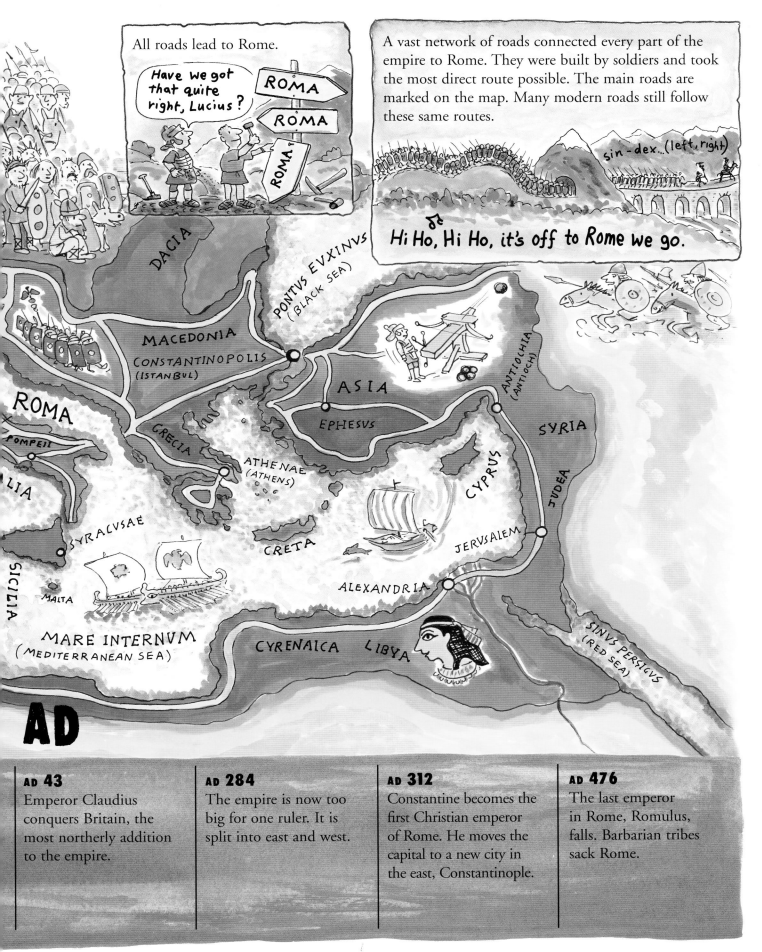

All roads lead to Rome.

A vast network of roads connected every part of the empire to Rome. They were built by soldiers and took the most direct route possible. The main roads are marked on the map. Many modern roads still follow these same routes.

AD

AD 43
Emperor Claudius conquers Britain, the most northerly addition to the empire.

AD 284
The empire is now too big for one ruler. It is split into east and west.

AD 312
Constantine becomes the first Christian emperor of Rome. He moves the capital to a new city in the east, Constantinople.

AD 476
The last emperor in Rome, Romulus, falls. Barbarian tribes sack Rome.

HOW TO MAKE A WATER CLOCK

Romans used sundials to tell the time. They were all right if it was sunny, but imagine trying to tell the time at night. For this Romans used a water clock (**clepsydra**). They still needed a sundial to mark out the time scale on the water clock.

TIP BOX
The time the water takes to drip through will depend on the size of the hole.

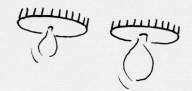

YOU'LL NEED:
A large plastic bottle with top, scissors, strong thumbtack, stopwatch, and marker.

Almost time for a drink of water.

Ancient clepsydra scale

 1 Ask an adult to help cut the bottle in two.

 2 Make a small hole in the bottle top using the thumbtack.

 3 Turn the top into the bottom.

 4 Pour some water into the top, and time how much water drips through in 1 minute, 2 minutes, 3 minutes, and so on.

Romans used them to time speeches.

Oh no! Another 15 clepsydra man.

 5 Mark the side, and make a scale of minutes.

Experiment with the size of the hole and bottle to make the most useful clock.

HOW TO MAKE A SHIELD

If you were a Roman soldier in battle, the only thing between you and your enemy's sword was your shield. It was made by sticking layers of wood together, and it was curved for strength. Inside was a leather handle protected on the outside by a metal boss.

TIP BOX
Glue the two pieces of cardboard together with the corrugation going in opposite ways. This makes it stronger.

Metal boss

Ask an adult to cut out two sheets of cardboard, 30 x 20 inches (75 x 50 cm).

2 Dampen the cardboard sheets with a spray (not too much!) and bend them.

3 Lay them over the plastic bottles to form a curve. Paint the tops with PVA mixed with an equal amount of water. Allow to dry.

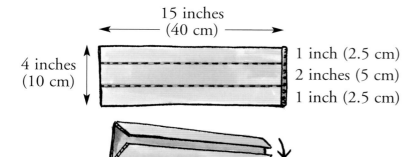

15 inches (40 cm)

4 inches (10 cm)

1 inch (2.5 cm)
2 inches (5 cm)
1 inch (2.5 cm)

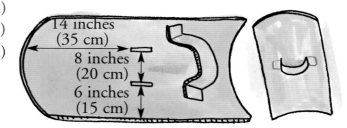

14 inches (35 cm)
8 inches (20 cm)
6 inches (15 cm)

4 Make a handle out of corrugated cardboard. Fold over and glue.

5 Make two 2-inch-long (5-cm) cuts in one curved sheet and insert the handle into them.

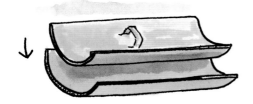

6 Fit both curved sheets together and glue.

7 Cut the bottom off one plastic bottle in a star shape.

8 Fold over the star points and glue to a sheet of thin cardboard. Stick this to the front of the shield.

9 Decorate with acrylic paint and stencils.

HOW TO MAKE A FORT

When the Romans conquered a new country, they had to defend themselves from constant attacks. They built strong forts as bases for Roman soldiers. In AD 122, the Emperor Hadrian had a wall built across northern Britain to stop attacks by barbarians from Scotland. It was 75 miles (120 km) long and 20 feet (6 m) high. It can still be seen today.

YOU'LL NEED:
Thin cardboard (cereal box), stencils, scissors, ruler, glue, pencil, and paints.

SOLDIERS SENT TO BRITAIN FROM WARM COUNTRIES FOUND IT VERY COLD. THEY PUT BITS OF SHEEP'S WOOL BETWEEN THEIR TOES TO KEEP THEM WARM.

TIP BOX
You can make longer walls by drawing them twice with the stencil.

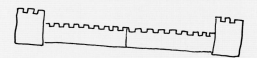

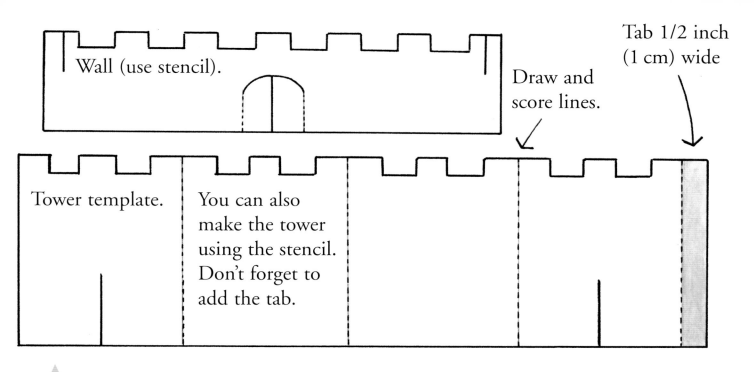

Wall (use stencil).

Draw and score lines.

Tab 1/2 inch (1 cm) wide

Tower template. You can also make the tower using the stencil. Don't forget to add the tab.

1 Draw the wall stencil onto cardboard. Cut it out. Copy the tower template onto cardboard. (See the instructions on the inside front cover.)

Glue tab here.

2 Cut out and fold the tower like this.

3 Cut a slit in the two sides of the tower that join the walls. Cut a slit in each top end of the wall.

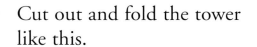

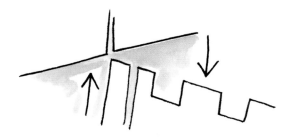

4 Join the walls to the tower by putting one slit into the other.

5 Join four walls and four towers in a square to make a fort. Draw and make a gate. Paint the fort to look like stone.

HOW TO MAKE A MEAL

In Rome, most people lived in small wooden apartments where cooking was banned as a fire hazard. They had to buy takeout from the local food bar called a **popina**. What a good name! Rich Romans ate a lot. They held enormous feasts where guests lay on couches and stuffed themselves. When they were full, they could make themselves sick and then continue partying.

BIG C's MORE-THAN-YOU-CAN-EAT BUFFET

Indigestion
Sometimes they weren't sure if they had eaten too much or been poisoned!

WERE SOME EMPERORS CRAZY? WE KNOW THAT WINE WAS HEATED AND FOOD WAS COOKED IN LEAD CONTAINERS. FROM WHAT WE KNOW TODAY ABOUT LEAD POISONING, PERHAPS THIS WASN'T A GOOD IDEA!

YOU HAVE TO BE MAD TO RULE HERE

They're coming to take me away . . . HA HA!

PANIS DULCIS (sweet bread)

GET AN ADULT TO HELP YOU WITH THIS.

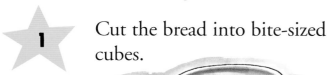

1 Cut the bread into bite-sized cubes.

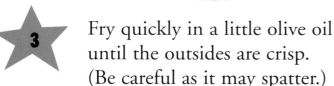

2 Dip them in milk.

Yum!

3 Fry quickly in a little olive oil until the outsides are crisp. (Be careful as it may spatter.)

4 Serve immediately with warmed honey.

ROMAN LENTILS

WE ARE USING A MICROWAVE OVEN. GET A MODERN ADULT TO HELP YOU WITH THIS ONE!

This recipe is based on an 800 W microwave oven.

Roman soldiers would cook it in an iron pot over a camp fire.

YOU'LL NEED:
2 1/2 ounces red lentils, 1 cup cold water, 1 tablespoon lemon juice, 1 teaspoon vinegar, 1/2 teaspoon freshly chopped coriander leaves, 1/4 teaspoon salt

This will serve 2 children or 1 large Roman soldier.

1 Put the lentils and water in a large bowl and cover.

2 Microwave on full power for 10 minutes.

3 Using oven mitts, take out the bowl and stir in the other ingedients.

4 Cook uncovered for 5 more minutes.

HOW TO GET A HOT BATH

These were not just places for a quick splash but somewhere to meet friends and chat. All Roman cities had public baths and toilets. There were separate ones for men and women.

YOU'LL NEED:
One Roman legion, 3,000 slaves, 1 1/2 square miles (4 sq km) of forest with long trees for scaffolding, and lots of stones or bricks.

ONE IN THREE NOT FREE
THE POPULATION OF ITALY WAS ABOUT SIX MILLION, AND TWO MILLION OF THOSE WERE SLAVES.

STAFF MOTTO
BUILD OR BE KILLED
MUCH OF THE BUILDING WORK WAS DONE BY SOLDIERS. IT KEPT THEM OUT OF MISCHIEF WHEN NO FIGHTING WAS GOING ON.

First build an aqueduct from the nearest mountains.

More ducts and lead pipes take the water to public baths and fountains. Only very rich people had their own water supply.

Drinking fountain

The aqueduct is built at a slight angle so that the water(s) (**aquae**) flows gently down a stone channel (**ductus**) into the city.

SMART!

PUBLIC BATHS

The water is heated in a large stone tank lined with lead.

Slave   Fire

Hypocaust (central heating) warm air flows under the floor and inside the walls.

Warm air

PUBLIC TOILETS

Turned out nice again.

Sponge sticks for wiping.

Waste water flows into the river.

HOW TO USE YOUR STENCILS

Cut or tear off the stencil sheet from the back of the book. Choose a shape, and place it over your paper. You may need to hold it in place with masking tape. Draw the outline with pencil. You can shade in the area with colored crayons or take off the stencil and carefully color in with paint or a felt-tip. Experiment with colors and surfaces.

Laying paper over a textured surface.

 1 Use your stencils to write Roman numbers and decorate your models.

TIP BOX

Put a light pencil mark on the paper as a guide to show where your stencil should go. Be sure not to let your stencil move.

Paint or color with felt-tips.

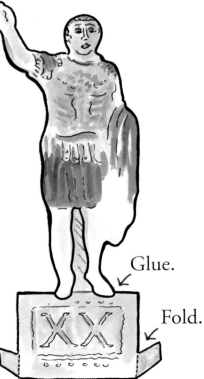

Glue.

Fold.